Reclaiming Your Time:
A Guide to Digital Balance

By

Frank Nwaorie

First Published in 2024 by Frank Nwaorie.

Table of Contents

Preface

My name is Frank Nwaorie, and I have witnessed firsthand the transformative power of digital technology, as well as its potential to consume our time and attention. Drawing on extensive research and personal experiences, I aim to shed light on the subtle ways in which the internet can dominate our lives and offer solutions to reclaim control over our time.

In today's hyper-connected world, the internet offers endless possibilities for learning, communication, and entertainment. However, it also presents a significant challenge which is finding a healthy balance between our online and offline lives. As our dependency on digital devices grows, so too does the risk of internet addiction, a phenomenon that affects both young and old alike.

"Reclaiming Your Time: A Guide to Digital Balance" is a comprehensive exploration of this modern dilemma.

This book is designed to help you understand the underlying causes of internet addiction and provide practical strategies to manage and mitigate its impact on your life.

Whether you're a teenager navigating social media pressures, a professional grappling with constant connectivity, or a parent concerned about your child's screen time, this guide offers valuable insights and actionable advice.

This book is divided into 5 major parts: Part I - Understanding Internet Addiction which highlights on Internet addiction, and its impact. Part II of this book delve into assessing your digital habits; self-assessment tools and understanding your triggers. The third part of this book reveals key strategies for digital balance, how to set healthy boundaries, being mindful of the use of technology and enhancing real-life connections.

The Part IV discusses on how to implement changes; creating a balanced digital routine, recommended tools and mobile apps for digital wellness and how best to do with relapses. The final part of this book Part V discusses on special considerations on digital balance for families, digital detox for professionals and lastly elderly and digital literacy.

Reclaiming Your Time: A Guide to Digital Balance will guide you through the steps to create healthier digital habits, cultivate mindfulness in your online interactions, and establish boundaries that protect your well-being. By understanding the psychological and social aspects of internet use, you will be better equipped to make informed decisions and foster a more balanced and fulfilling life.

It is my hope that this book, will serve as a valuable resource for anyone seeking to navigate the complexities of the digital age with intention and awareness.

Together, we can learn to harness the benefits of technology while preserving the precious moments of our offline lives.

You have made the greatest choice to have read this book.

Sincerely,

Frank Nwaorie

Acknowledgments

The journey of writing this book has been both challenging and rewarding. I would like to express my gratitude to the researchers and experts whose work has contributed to the understanding of internet addiction and digital balance. Special thanks go to my family and friends for their unwavering support and patience throughout this process.

It is my hope that "Reclaiming Your Time: A Guide to Digital Balance" will inspire and empower you to take control of your digital habits and lead a more fulfilling life. Together, we can navigate the complexities of the digital age with intention and awareness.

Introduction

The Rise of Digital Dependency

In the past few decades, the internet has revolutionized the way we live, work, and interact with one another. From instant communication through social media and email to endless information at our fingertips, the digital age has brought about unprecedented convenience and connectivity. However, with these advancements comes a growing concern: digital dependency.

Digital dependency, or internet addiction, is characterized by excessive and compulsive use of the internet that interferes with daily life. This phenomenon has become increasingly prevalent across all age groups, leading to a host of physical, mental, and social consequences. According to a study published in the Journal of Behavioural Addictions, internet addiction affects approximately 6% of the global population, with higher rates observed in adolescents and young adults.

Purpose of This Book

"Reclaiming Your Time: A Guide to Digital Balance" aims to address the pervasive issue of internet addiction by providing readers with the tools and strategies needed to achieve a healthier relationship with digital technology. This book is designed to be a comprehensive resource for individuals of all ages who are seeking to regain control over their time and attention in an increasingly digital world.

Through a combination of research-based insights and practical advice, this guide will help you understand the root causes of internet addiction, recognize its impact on various aspects of your life, and implement effective strategies to foster digital balance. Whether you are a parent concerned about your child's screen time, a professional struggling with constant connectivity, or someone simply looking to make more mindful choices, this book offers valuable guidance tailored to your needs.

How to Use This Book

The journey to digital balance is a deeply personal one, and there is no one-size-fits-all solution. This book is structured to provide flexibility, allowing you to focus on the sections that resonate most with your unique circumstances. Here's how you can navigate the content:

Start with Self-Assessment: Begin by evaluating your current digital habits and identifying any problematic patterns. This will provide a baseline for tracking your progress and tailoring the strategies to your needs.

Explore the Causes and Effects: Gain a deeper understanding of what drives internet addiction and how it impacts your physical health, mental well-being, and social relationships.

Implement Practical Strategies: Discover a variety of techniques for setting boundaries, practicing digital mindfulness, and enhancing your offline life. Choose the strategies that align with your lifestyle and goals.

Address Special Considerations: If you belong to a specific demographic, such as families with children, professionals, or seniors, explore the dedicated sections that offer tailored advice for your situation.

Utilize the Appendices: Make use of the additional resources, support services, and self-help tools provided in the appendices to further aid your journey.

Following this guide, will ensure you are equipped with the knowledge and tools necessary to create a balanced digital routine that enhances your overall well-being. Remember, the goal is not to eliminate digital technology from your life, but to use it in a way that supports and enriches your daily experiences.

Part I:

Understanding Internet

Addiction

Chapter 1

What is Internet Addiction?

Definition and Overview

Internet addiction, also known as problematic internet use or compulsive internet use, is a behavioural addiction characterized by excessive or poorly controlled preoccupations, urges, or behaviours regarding internet use that lead to impairment or distress.

Dr. Kimberly Young, one of the pioneering researchers in this field, defines internet addiction as a clinical disorder with symptoms similar to other addictions, such as compulsive behaviour, withdrawal, tolerance, and negative repercussions on daily functioning (Young, 1998).

Internet addiction can occur through the followings:

Gaming addiction: Which is excessive engagement in online video games.

Social media addiction: Which means compulsive use of social networking websites.

Information overload: Which is referred to as constant web surfing or database searching.

Online shopping and auction addiction: An uncontrolled buying or bidding on e-commerce platforms.

Signs and Symptoms

Recognizing the signs of internet addiction is crucial for early intervention.

We shall discuss the following common symptoms below:

Preoccupation with the internet
This is the constantly thinking about being online, even when not using it.

Increased use over time

This is abusive us or rather spending more time online to achieve satisfaction or excitement.

Failed attempts to control use

This means unsuccessful efforts to cut down or stop using the internet.

Withdrawal symptoms

Victims are likely to experiencing irritability, anxiety, or depression when not online.

Neglect of other activities

Internet addicts tend to ignore social, occupational, or recreational activities in favour of internet use.

Continued use despite problems

There are worse cases of victims persisting with internet use despite awareness of its negative impact on one's life.

The Psychology behind Internet Addiction

Internet addiction shares commonalities with other behavioural addictions. According to Dr. Mark Griffiths, a prominent psychologist in addiction studies, the psychological mechanisms behind internet addiction include:

Reward System Activation:

The brain's reward system, involving dopamine release, is stimulated by online activities, reinforcing the behaviour.

Escapism:

The internet provides a means to escape real-life stressors and problems, leading to increased reliance on online activities.

Social Interactions:

Online platforms offer social validation and a sense of belonging, which can be particularly appealing to those with social anxiety or low self-esteem.

Chapter 2

The Impact of Internet Addiction

Physical Health Consequences

Prolonged internet use can lead to several physical health issues:

Eye Strain and Vision Problems

Extended screen time can cause digital eye strain, characterized by dryness, irritation, and blurred vision (Sheppard & Wolffsohn, 2018).

Poor Posture and Musculoskeletal Problems

Sitting for long periods can lead to poor posture, back pain, and repetitive strain injuries (Shariat et al., 2018).

Sleep Disorders

Excessive internet use, especially before bedtime, can disrupt sleep patterns and lead to insomnia (Hershner & Chervin, 2014).

Mental Health Implications

Internet addiction is associated with various mental health issues, including:

Depression and Anxiety

Studies have shown a strong correlation between excessive internet use and increased levels of depression and anxiety (Lin et al., 2016).

Loneliness and Social Isolation

Despite the internet's potential for social connectivity, heavy users often report feelings of loneliness and isolation (Kraut et al., 1998).

Attention Deficit and Impulse Control

Internet addiction can impair cognitive functions such as attention span, memory, and impulse control (Swing et al., 2010).

Social and Relationship Effects

Internet addiction can strain personal relationships and social life. The following effects are discussed briefly below:

Family Conflicts

Excessive online activities can lead to neglect of family responsibilities and conflicts with loved ones (Cheng & Li, 2014).

Workplace Issues

Internet addiction can result in decreased productivity, absenteeism, and job loss due to time spent online instead of working (Young, 2004).

Academic Problems

Students with internet addiction often show a decline in academic performance and attendance (Kuss et al., 2014).

Having a good knowledge of this multifaceted impact of internet addiction on physical, mental, and social health is the first step toward addressing this pervasive issue.

Now that you have this first hand information we shall in the next part of this book explore how to assess your digital habits and recognize the triggers that contribute to problematic internet use.

Part II:

Assessing Your Digital Habits

Chapter 3

Self-Assessment Tools

Before you set in into the journey to strike digital balance, it is essential to evaluate your current digital habits and recognize any problematic patterns. In this chapter we shall discuss on the provisions of self-assessment tools to help you understand your internet usage and identify areas that may require change.

Evaluating Your Screen Time

One of the first steps in assessing your digital habits is to evaluate how much time you spend on your digital devices. Tracking screen time can provide insights into your usage patterns and highlight areas where you may need to cut back.

Tracking Apps and Tools

Numerous apps and tools can help you monitor your screen time across various devices. Some popular options include:

Screen Time (iOS):

This is a built-in feature on iPhones, iPads or any other iOS enabled devices. Screen Time tracks the amount of time you spend on apps and websites.

Digital Wellbeing (Android):

This app helps you understand and manage your digital habits on Android devices.

RescueTime:

This is a comprehensive tool that tracks your activity on computers and mobile devices, providing detailed reports on how you spend your time.

Using these tools will help you track your screen time for at least a week to enable you get an accurate picture of your daily usage.

Having revealed the tools above, kindly pay attention to the following:

Total Screen Time

This means the cumulative time spent on all digital devices.

App and Website Usage

This simply means the amount of time spent on specific apps and websites.

Frequency of Use

This depicts how often you check your devices throughout the day.

Peak Usage Times

It means the times of day when your screen time is highest.

Setting Goals

Once you have a clear understanding of your screen time, set specific goals to reduce it. For example, aim to limit your social media usage to one hour per day or designate certain times of the day as screen-free zones. Research suggests that setting clear, achievable goals can significantly improve self-regulation and reduce problematic internet use (Hofmann et al., 2012).

Recognizing Problematic Patterns

In addition to evaluating screen time, it is important to recognize patterns that may indicate problematic internet use. Reflecting on your digital habits can help you identify triggers and behaviours that contribute to excessive use.

Common Problematic Patterns

Compulsive Checking:

Feeling the urge to check your phone or social media accounts frequently, even when there are no notifications.

Neglecting Responsibilities:

Prioritizing internet use over essential tasks such as work, studies, or household chores.

Using the Internet as a Coping Mechanism:

Turning to the internet to escape stress, boredom, or negative emotions.

Social Isolation:

Spending more time interacting online than engaging in face-to-face interactions with family and friends.

Self-Reflection Questions

To gain deeper insights into your digital habits, these are the questions to ask yourself:

Do I feel anxious or irritable when I cannot access the internet?

Have I tried to reduce my screen time but failed?

Do I use the internet to avoid dealing with real-life problems or emotions?

Has my internet use negatively impacted my relationships, work, or studies?

Do I lose track of time when I am online, often spending longer than intended?

If you answer "yes" to several of these questions, it may indicate that you have problematic internet use. Recognizing these patterns is the first step toward making positive changes.

Advanced Professional Assessment Tools

For a more comprehensive assessment, consider using standardized questionnaires and scales developed by experts in the field. Some widely used tools include:

Internet Addiction Test (IAT): Developed by Dr. Kimberly Young, the IAT is a 20-item questionnaire that assesses the severity of internet addiction (Young, 1998).

Compulsive Internet Use Scale (CIUS): A 14-item scale that measures the degree of compulsive internet use and its impact on daily life (Meerkerk et al., 2009).

These tools can provide a more detailed understanding of your digital habits and help you identify specific areas for improvement.

Chapter 4

Understanding Your Triggers

To effectively manage and reduce internet addiction, it is essential to understand the underlying triggers that drive excessive internet use. This chapter focuses on identifying both emotional and situational triggers, as well as exploring the significant role of social media and instant gratification in fostering addictive behaviours.

Identifying Emotional and Situational Triggers

Emotional Triggers

Emotions play a crucial role in shaping our online behaviours. Many individuals turn to the internet as a coping mechanism to manage various emotional states.

Common emotional triggers include:

Stress and Anxiety

The internet offers a temporary escape from the pressures of everyday life. Online activities such as browsing social media, watching videos, or playing games can provide a distraction from stress and anxiety.

However, this reliance can lead to a cycle of avoidance and increased stress over time (Caplan, 2007).

Boredom

When feeling bored, people often use the internet to pass the time and seek stimulation. The vast array of online content can provide a quick fix for boredom, making it a habitual response (Lam & Peng, 2010).

Loneliness and Social Isolation

The internet can serve as a substitute for real-life social interactions, offering a sense of connection through social media and online communities. This can be particularly appealing for individuals who feel lonely or socially isolated (Kraut et al., 1998).

Depression

Individuals experiencing depressive symptoms may use the internet to distract themselves from negative thoughts and feelings. However, excessive internet use can exacerbate depression by reducing face-to-face interactions and increasing feelings of isolation (Lin et al., 2016).

Situational Triggers

In addition to emotional triggers, situational factors can also influence internet use.

Understanding these triggers can help someone develop strategies to manage them effectively:

Environmental Factors

Access to digital devices and the internet at all times can make it challenging to limit usage. Creating a physical environment that supports healthy digital habits, such as designated screen-free zones, can be beneficial.

Time of Day

Certain times of day, such as late at night, can be more conducive to excessive internet use. Establishing a routine and setting specific times for internet use can help manage this trigger.

Social Influences

Peer pressure and social norms can impact internet use. For example, if your friends or colleagues are constantly online, you may feel compelled to do the same.

Setting personal boundaries and communicating them to others can help mitigate this influence.

The Role of Social Media and Instant Gratification

Social Media as a Trigger

Social media platforms are designed to capture and hold our attention, often leading to compulsive use.

Several factors contribute to this phenomenon:

Intermittent Reinforcement

Social media platforms use intermittent reinforcement, where rewards (likes, comments, shares) are given at unpredictable intervals. This creates a sense of anticipation and keeps users engaged, similar to gambling behaviours (Montag et al., 2019).

Social Validation

Social media provides immediate feedback through likes and comments, which can boost self-esteem and create a sense of social validation. This feedback loop can make users crave more interactions, leading to increased usage (Andreassen et al., 2017).

Fear of Missing Out (FOMO)

The constant stream of updates and notifications can create a fear of missing out on important events or information. This can drive individuals to check their social media accounts frequently (Przybylski et al., 2013).

Instant Gratification and Its Effects

The internet offers immediate rewards and instant gratification, which can reinforce addictive behaviours.

The need for instant gratification can undermine self-control and lead to excessive internet use in several ways:

Instant Access to Information and Entertainment

The internet provides instant access to a vast array of information and entertainment options. This can create an expectation of immediate satisfaction and make it difficult to tolerate delays or engage in more effortful activities (Carr, 2010).

Reduced Patience and Attention Span

Constant exposure to fast-paced online content can reduce patience and shorten attention spans. This can make it challenging to engage in activities that require sustained focus and effort (Wilson, 2014).

Impulsive Behaviours

The immediate rewards offered by the internet can encourage impulsive behaviours, such as compulsive shopping or binge-watching videos.

These behaviours can become habitual and difficult to control over time (Billieux et al., 2015).

Understanding the emotional and situational triggers, along with the role of social media and instant gratification, is essential for developing strategies to manage internet use. Thus, recognizing and addressing these triggers, you can create healthier digital habits and achieve a more balanced life.

Part III:

Strategies for

Digital Balance

Chapter 5

Setting Healthy Boundaries

Achieving digital balance requires setting healthy boundaries around your internet use. This chapter explores practical strategies to help you create a digital detox plan and establish screen-free zones and times, allowing you to reclaim your time and improve your overall well-being.

Creating a Digital Detox Plan

Understanding the Importance of Digital Detox

A digital detox involves taking a break from digital devices to reduce stress, increase mindfulness, and reconnect with the physical world. Research has shown that taking regular breaks from technology can improve mental health, enhance focus, and foster better relationships (Wilmer, Sherman, & Chein, 2017).

Steps to Create a Digital Detox Plan

Assess Your Current Usage:

Begin by tracking your screen time to understand your digital habits. Use tools like Screen Time (iOS), Digital Wellbeing (Android), or RescueTime to gather data on how much time you spend on different apps and websites.

Set Clear Goals:

Define what you hope to achieve with your digital detox. Goals may include reducing stress, improving sleep, spending more time with loved ones, or increasing productivity. Make sure your goals are specific, measurable, achievable, relevant, and time-bound (SMART).

Plan Your Detox Period:

Decide on the duration of your detox. It could range from a few hours each day to an entire weekend or even longer. Choose a period that feels challenging yet manageable. According to Dr. Hilarie Cash, co-founder of the reSTART

Center for Digital Technology Sustainability, even short breaks can have significant benefits if done consistently (Cash et al., 2012).

Identify Triggers and Replace Activities:

Recognize the triggers that lead to excessive internet use. Replace digital activities with offline alternatives that you enjoy, such as reading, exercising, cooking, or spending time in nature.

Inform Others and Seek Support:

Let friends, family, and colleagues know about your digital detox plan. Their support and understanding can help you stay committed. You might also consider detoxing with a friend or family member for added motivation.

Create a Schedule:

Plan your day to include specific times for offline activities. This can help you avoid the temptation to go online. Structure your schedule to balance work, leisure, and social interactions without digital interference.

Evaluate and Adjust:

After completing your detox period, reflect on the experience. Assess how it impacted your well-being and identify any challenges you faced. Use these insights to adjust your digital habits and incorporate regular detox periods into your routine.

Establishing Screen-Free Zones and Times

The Benefits of Screen-Free Zones and Times

Creating designated screen-free zones and times can help you develop healthier digital habits, improve focus, and foster deeper connections with others. Research indicates that setting physical and temporal boundaries around technology use can reduce distractions and enhance productivity (Mark, Gudith, & Klocke, 2008).

Steps to Establish Screen-Free Zones

Identify Key Areas:

Choose areas in your home where screens will be restricted. Common screen-free zones include the bedroom, dining room, and family room. According to the American Academy of Pediatrics, keeping screens out of these areas can promote better sleep and encourage family interactions (AAP, 2016).

Remove Devices:

Physically remove digital devices from these zones. This includes smart phones, tablets, laptops, and televisions. Store them in a designated area away from the screen-free zones to reduce temptation.

Create a Welcoming Environment:

Make the screen-free zones inviting and conducive to offline activities. Add comfortable seating, good lighting, books, board games, or other items that encourage relaxation and engagement without screens.

Establish Rules:

Set clear rules for screen-free zones and communicate them to everyone in the household. For example, no devices allowed during meals or after a certain time in the evening.

Steps to Establish Screen-Free Times

Designate Specific Times:

Identify specific times of day when you will avoid using screens. Common screen-free times include during meals, an hour before bed, or the first hour after waking up. Research by the National Sleep Foundation suggests that reducing screen time before bed can improve sleep quality (NSF, 2011).

Set Boundaries for Work and Leisure:

Differentiate between work-related and leisure screen time. Allocate specific times for checking emails and working online, and ensure that you have ample screen-free time for relaxation and social interactions.

Use Technology Wisely:

Utilize features on your devices to support screen-free times. Set "Do Not Disturb" modes, schedule downtime, or use apps that limit your usage during designated periods.

Engage in Offline Activities:

Plan engaging offline activities during screen-free times to make the transition easier. Consider hobbies, physical exercise, social gatherings, or outdoor adventures.

Be Consistent:

Consistency is key to establishing new habits. Stick to your screen-free times even when it feels challenging. Over time, these periods will become a natural part of your routine.

Creating a digital detox plan and establishing screen-free zones and times, is a sure win you can take significant steps toward achieving digital balance. These strategies will help you reclaim your time, reduce stress, and foster meaningful connections in your offline life.

CHAPTER 6

Mindful Use of Technology

In today's hyper-connected world, practicing mindful technology use is essential for achieving digital balance and maintaining overall well-being. This chapter explores the principles of digital mindfulness and offers practical techniques for conscious consumption of digital content.

Practicing Digital Mindfulness

Understanding Digital Mindfulness

Digital mindfulness involves being fully present and aware while using technology. It means engaging with digital devices intentionally and purposefully, rather than mindlessly scrolling or multitasking. By practicing digital mindfulness, you can enhance your focus, reduce stress, and create a healthier relationship with technology (Davis & Hayes, 2011).

Principles of Digital Mindfulness

Awareness:

Recognize when and why you are using digital devices. Pay attention to your habits and how they impact your mood, productivity, and relationships.

Intention:

Use technology with a clear purpose. Before reaching for your phone or opening an app, ask yourself what you intend to achieve and whether it aligns with your goals.

Presence:

Stay present in the moment while using digital devices. Avoid multitasking and focus on one task at a time. This can improve your efficiency and enjoyment of the activity.

Reflection:

Regularly reflect on your digital habits. Assess whether your technology use supports your values and well-being, and make adjustments as needed.

Steps to Practice Digital Mindfulness

Set Clear Intentions:

Before using a digital device, set a clear intention. For example, if you are checking your email, decide how much time you will spend and what you hope to accomplish.

Take Breaks:

Incorporate regular breaks into your digital activities. Follow the 20-20-20 rule: every 20 minutes, take a 20-second break and look at something 20 feet away. This can reduce eye strain and help you stay mindful (Rosenfield, 2011).

Limit Multitasking:

Focus on one digital task at a time. Avoid switching between multiple apps or devices, as this can reduce your productivity and increase stress (Ophir, Nass, & Wagner, 2009).

Practice Gratitude:

Cultivate a sense of gratitude for the benefits that technology provides. Acknowledging the positive aspects of digital tools can help you use them more mindfully and appreciate their value without becoming overly dependent on them.

Create Digital Rituals:

Establish rituals around your technology use. For example, start your day with a mindful morning routine that includes checking emails or social media at specific times, rather than sporadically throughout the day.

Techniques for Conscious Consumption

Understanding Conscious Consumption

Conscious consumption involves being selective and intentional about the digital content you engage with. It means choosing quality over quantity and prioritizing content that enriches your life and aligns with your values (Vogel et al., 2014).

Techniques for Conscious Consumption

Curate Your Feed:

Take control of the content you consume by curating your social media feeds and subscriptions. Follow accounts and sources that inspire, educate, and uplift you, and unfollow or mute those that cause stress or negativity.

Set Content Boundaries:

Establish boundaries around the types of content you consume. Limit exposure to news, social media, or entertainment that triggers negative emotions or contributes to information overload.

Schedule Content Consumption:

Allocate specific times for consuming digital content, such as reading the news or browsing social media. Avoid consuming content mindlessly throughout the day, which can lead to distraction and reduced productivity (Chun et al., 2011).

Engage with Purpose:

When consuming digital content, engage with it purposefully. Reflect on why you are consuming the content and what you hope to gain from it. This can help you make more intentional choices about what to watch, read, or listen to.

Practice Digital Minimalism:

Adopt a minimalist approach to your digital life by reducing the number of apps, subscriptions, and digital accounts you maintain. Focus on essential tools and content that genuinely add value to your life (Newport, 2019).

Be Present:

When consuming digital content, be fully present. Avoid multitasking and give your full attention to the content. This can enhance your understanding and enjoyment of the material.

Mindful Browsing and Scrolling

Limit Scrolling:

Set a timer when browsing or scrolling through social media to prevent getting lost in endless content. Once the timer goes off, take a break or switch to a different activity.

Pause and Reflect:

Before liking, sharing, or commenting on content, take a moment to reflect on why you are doing it and how it aligns with your values.

Engage Mindfully:

Interact with content that truly resonates with you and avoid engaging in meaningless interactions that can drain your energy and time.

Mindful Communication

Choose Quality over Quantity:

Focus on having meaningful interactions online rather than numerous superficial ones. Prioritize conversations that foster genuine connections and enrich your relationships.

Be Present in Conversations:

When communicating digitally, be fully present. Avoid multitasking and give your full attention to the person you are interacting with.

Practicing digital mindfulness and employing techniques for conscious consumption can create a healthier relationship with technology. The strategies discussed in this chapter will help you stay focused, reduce stress, and ensure that your digital activities align with your values and goals.

Chapter 7

Enhancing Real-Life Connections

This chapter explores the importance of prioritizing face-to-face interactions and reconnecting with offline hobbies and interests. This is so necessary because in an era dominated by digital communication, enhancing real-life connections is crucial for maintaining mental health and fostering meaningful relationships.

Prioritizing Face-to-Face Interactions

The Importance of Face-to-Face Interactions

Face-to-face interactions are vital for developing strong social bonds and emotional well-being. Research has shown that in-person communication is more effective in conveying emotions and building trust compared to digital communication (Turkle, 2015).

Nonverbal cues such as facial expressions, body language, and tone of voice play a significant role in understanding and connecting with others.

Benefits of Face-to-Face Interactions

Enhanced Emotional Connection:

In-person interactions allow for deeper emotional connections. Studies indicate that face-to-face communication releases oxytocin, a hormone associated with bonding and trust (Dunbar, 2010).

Improved Mental Health:

Regular face-to-face interactions are linked to lower levels of depression and anxiety. Social connections act as a buffer against stress and provide a sense of belonging (Holt-Lunstad, Smith, & Layton, 2010).

Better Conflict Resolution:

In-person interactions facilitate better conflict resolution as they allow for immediate feedback and a more nuanced understanding of the other person's perspective (Gottman & Silver, 1999).

Strategies to Prioritize Face-to-Face Interactions

Schedule Regular Meet-Ups:

Make it a habit to schedule regular face-to-face meetings with friends and family. Whether it's a weekly coffee date or a monthly dinner, consistent in-person interactions can strengthen relationships.

Limit Digital Interference:

When spending time with others, minimize digital distractions. Put away smart phones and focus on being present in the moment. This shows respect and attentiveness, enhancing the quality of the interaction (Newport, 2019).

Engage in Group Activities:

Join clubs, groups, or community events that align with your interests. Group activities provide opportunities to meet new people and build social networks.

Practice Active Listening:

Engage in active listening during face-to-face interactions. This involves fully concentrating on the speaker, understanding their message, responding thoughtfully, and remembering the conversation (Brownell, 2012).

Use Technology to Facilitate In-Person Meetings:

While technology can sometimes hinder real-life connections, it can also be used to facilitate them. Use digital tools to arrange and coordinate in-person meet-ups and activities.

Reconnecting with Offline Hobbies and Interests

The Value of Offline Hobbies

Engaging in offline hobbies and interests is essential for personal growth, creativity, and relaxation. Offline activities provide a break from screen time, reduce stress, and offer opportunities for skill development and social interaction.

Benefits of Offline Hobbies

Stress Reduction:

Participating in hobbies such as gardening, painting, or playing sports can reduce stress and promote relaxation. These activities often require focus and mindfulness, which can provide a mental break from daily pressures (Pressman et al., 2009).

Enhanced Creativity:

Engaging in creative activities like writing, drawing, or crafting stimulates the brain and enhances problem-solving skills. Creativity can also improve mental health and overall well-being (Csikszentmihalyi, 1996).

Physical Health Benefits:

Physical hobbies such as hiking, dancing, or playing sports contribute to physical fitness and overall health. Regular physical activity is linked to reduced risk of chronic diseases and improved mental health (Warburton, Nicol, & Bredin, 2006).

Social Interaction:

Many hobbies involve group activities or communities. Joining a book club, sports team, or art class can provide social interaction and opportunities to meet like-minded individuals.

Strategies to Reconnect with Offline Hobbies

Identify Your Interests:

Reflect on your passions and interests. Consider activities you enjoyed in the past or new hobbies you'd like to explore. Make a list of potential hobbies and prioritize those that excite you the most.

Allocate Time for Hobbies:

Set aside dedicated time each week for your hobbies. Treat this time as non-negotiable and prioritize it just as you would any other important appointment.

Join Groups or Classes:

Having discussed this earlier, look for local clubs, classes, or groups related to your hobbies. Engaging in these activities with others can provide motivation and a sense of community.

Limit Screen Time:

Reduce time spent on digital devices to make room for offline activities. Set boundaries for screen time and use that time to engage in your hobbies instead (Newport, 2019).

Create a Hobby-Friendly Environment:

Designate a space in your home for your hobbies. Whether it's a corner for painting, a garden for plants, or a space for exercise, having a dedicated area can make it easier to engage in your hobbies regularly.

Incorporate Hobbies into Daily Life:

Find ways to incorporate your hobbies into your daily routine. For example, listen to audio books while commuting, take a walk during lunch breaks, or practice yoga in the morning.

Prioritizing face-to-face interactions and reconnecting with offline hobbies and interests can enhance your real-life connections and achieve a healthier balance between your digital and offline lives.

These strategies will not only improve your mental and physical well-being but also enrich your personal relationships and overall quality of life.

Part IV:

Implementing Change

Chapter 8

Creating A Balanced Digital Routine

Achieving a balanced digital routine is essential for maintaining mental and physical well-being. This chapter focuses on building a sustainable daily schedule and balancing work, leisure, and digital time, ensuring that technology serves as a tool for enhancing life rather than a source of distraction or stress.

Building a Sustainable Daily Schedule

Understanding the Importance of Routine

A well-structured routine provides stability, reduces stress, and enhances productivity. According to research, having a daily routine can improve mental health, increase efficiency, and provide a sense of control (Kabat-Zinn, 1990).

In the context of digital balance, a sustainable schedule helps in managing screen time effectively and ensures that technology use is purposeful and intentional.

Steps to Build a Sustainable Daily Schedule

Assess Your Current Routine:

Start by analyzing how you currently spend your time. Use time-tracking tools or keep a daily journal to identify patterns and areas where you might be overusing digital devices.

Set Priorities:

Determine your priorities for work, personal life, and leisure. Make sure your schedule reflects these priorities, allocating time for essential tasks, relaxation, and social interactions.

Designate Specific Times for Digital Activities:

Allocate specific times of the day for checking emails, social media, and other digital activities. Avoid random or continuous checking, which can lead to distraction and reduce productivity (Mark, Gudith, & Klocke, 2008).

Incorporate Breaks and Offline Activities:

Schedule regular breaks throughout your day to rest and recharge. Incorporate offline activities, such as reading, exercising, or spending time outdoors, to provide a balance to screen time.

Create Evening and Morning Routines:

Establish routines for the beginning and end of your day that minimize screen time. Start your day with activities that energize you, such as meditation or exercise, and end your day with relaxing activities like reading or journaling to improve sleep quality (National Sleep Foundation, 2011).

Use Technology to Support Your Routine:

Leverage digital tools and apps that help manage your time and stay organized. Tools like calendars, task managers, and screen time trackers can support your efforts to build a sustainable schedule.

Be Flexible and Adjust:

Life is unpredictable, and sometimes routines need to be adjusted. Be flexible and willing to adapt your schedule as needed while maintaining your overall goals for digital balance.

Balancing Work, Leisure, and Digital Time

The Importance of Balance

Balancing work, leisure, and digital time is crucial for preventing burnout and maintaining a healthy lifestyle.

Excessive screen time, especially for work-related tasks, can lead to stress, eye strain, and decreased productivity. Conversely, inadequate leisure time can affect mental health and overall well-being (Sonnentag, 2001).

Strategies for Balancing Work, Leisure, and Digital Time

Set Clear Boundaries:

Repeating this rule is intentional. Establish clear boundaries between work and personal time. Define specific working hours and stick to them. Avoid checking work emails or completing tasks outside of these hours to maintain a healthy work-life balance (Derks, van Mierlo, & Schmitz, 2014).

Prioritize Leisure Activities:

Make leisure activities a priority in your daily schedule. Engage in hobbies and activities that you enjoy and that provide relaxation and fulfilment.

Ensure that these activities are part of your routine and not pushed aside by digital distractions.

Limit Multitasking:

Avoid multitasking with digital devices, as it can reduce productivity and increase stress. Focus on one task at a time, whether it's work, leisure, or digital activities, to improve efficiency and enjoyment (Ophir, Nass, & Wagner, 2009).

Practice Time Management:

Use time management techniques such as the Pomodoro Technique or time blocking to allocate specific periods for work, digital activities, and leisure. These techniques can help you stay focused and ensure that you dedicate adequate time to each area of your life (Cirillo, 2006).

Create Digital-Free Zones and Times:

Designate certain areas of your home or specific times of the day as digital-free. For example, make the dining room a digital-free zone to encourage family interactions during meals, or establish a digital-free hour before bedtime to promote better sleep (Turkle, 2015).

Reflect and Adjust:

Regularly reflect on your digital habits and overall routine. Assess whether your current balance is working for you and make adjustments as needed. Continuously strive for a routine that supports your well-being and goals.

Incorporating Mindfulness

Mindful Breaks:

Take mindful breaks throughout your day to disconnect from screens and reconnect with yourself. Practice deep breathing, meditation, or simply take a walk to clear your mind.

Mindful Transitions:

Transition mindfully between work and leisure activities. Take a few moments to reflect and set intentions for the next part of your day, ensuring a clear separation between different aspects of your routine.

Building a sustainable daily schedule and balancing work, leisure, and digital time, can create a healthier relationship with technology. These strategies will help you manage screen time effectively, enhance productivity, and ensure that your digital activities support your overall well-being and life goals.

Chapter 9

Tools and Apps for Digital Wellness

As we navigate a digital world, leveraging technology to support digital wellness is crucial. This chapter focuses on utilizing technology to combat addiction and recommends apps and software designed to promote healthier digital habits.

Utilizing Technology to Combat Addiction

The Paradox of Technology

Technology, while often the source of digital addiction, can also provide solutions for managing and mitigating its effects. By using specific tools and apps, individuals can gain insights into their digital habits, set boundaries, and cultivate healthier relationships with their devices.

Behavioural Insights and Self-Monitoring

Understanding and monitoring one's digital habits is the first step toward achieving digital wellness. Numerous tools can provide detailed reports on screen time, app usage, and even the number of times a device is picked up throughout the day. This data can help identify problematic patterns and areas for improvement (Rosen, 2012).

Setting Boundaries with Technology

Screen Time Trackers:

Tools like Apple's Screen Time and Google's Digital Wellbeing offer comprehensive insights into how much time is spent on various apps and websites. They also allow users to set daily limits for specific apps or categories, helping to reduce excessive use.

App Blockers:

Apps like Freedom and StayFocusd enable users to block distracting websites and apps during designated times. This can be particularly useful for enhancing productivity and reducing the temptation to engage in mindless scrolling (Newport, 2019).

Mindfulness and Meditation Apps

Mindfulness and meditation apps can play a significant role in combating digital addiction. These apps encourage users to take regular breaks, practice mindfulness, and focus on their well-being.

Headspace:

This app offers guided meditation sessions tailored to various needs, including reducing stress and improving focus. It also includes features like mindful moments, which remind users to take breaks from their screens (Puddicombe, 2016).

Calm:

Calm provides meditation, sleep stories, and breathing exercises designed to promote relaxation and reduce anxiety. Its emphasis on mindfulness can help users develop a healthier relationship with technology (Tsekleves & Cooper, 2017).

Recommended Apps and Software

Apps for Digital Wellbeing

A variety of apps and software are specifically designed to help users manage their digital lives more effectively. Below are some of the most recommended tools for promoting digital wellness:

Moment:

Moment tracks how much time you spend on your phone and which apps you use the most.

It also offers a coaching program to help reduce screen time and develop healthier habits.

Forest:

Forest is a unique app that gamifies staying focused. Users plant virtual trees that grow when they avoid using their phones. If they leave the app, the tree dies, encouraging sustained focus and reduced screen time.

RescueTime:

RescueTime runs in the background on your computer and mobile devices, tracking time spent on various applications and websites. It provides detailed reports and allows users to set goals for productive time.

Tools for Focus and Productivity

Freedom:

Freedom blocks distracting websites and apps across all your devices. You can create customized blocklists and schedule focus sessions to help maintain productivity.

StayFocusd:

StayFocusd is a Chrome extension that restricts the amount of time you can spend on time-wasting websites. Once your allotted time is used up, the sites are blocked for the rest of the day.

Focus@Will:

This app uses specially curated music to improve concentration and productivity. The music is designed to keep your brain engaged while minimizing distractions.

Wellness and Lifestyle Apps

Fabulous:

Fabulous is a habit-building app that helps users develop healthy routines. It offers personalized coaching to improve sleep, nutrition, exercise, and productivity.

Habitica:

Habitica turns habit-building into a game, where users can earn rewards and level up by completing daily tasks and goals. It adds an element of fun to managing digital habits and encourages consistency.

Streaks:

Streaks is a habit-tracking app that helps users form good habits by encouraging them to maintain streaks of daily activity. It's useful for building consistent routines and reducing dependence on digital devices.

Tools for Parents and Families

OurPact:

OurPact is a parental control app that allows parents to manage their children's screen time by setting schedules, blocking apps, and tracking usage. It helps ensure a balanced approach to technology for younger users.

Circle:

Circle provides comprehensive parental controls for managing screen time and online content. It allows parents to set limits, filter content, and monitor activity across all connected devices in the household.

In summary, using technology to combat addiction and employing recommended apps and software, individuals can develop healthier digital habits and achieve better balance in their lives.

Chapter 10

Dealing With Relapses

Establishing a balanced digital routine is an ongoing journey that may include relapses. Recognizing and addressing setbacks is crucial for long-term success. This chapter explores how to identify setbacks and provides strategies to maintain digital wellness over time.

Recognizing and Addressing Setbacks

Understanding Relapses

A relapse, in the context of digital wellness, refers to reverting to previous unhealthy digital habits after a period of improvement. Relapses can occur for various reasons, such as stress, boredom, or environmental triggers. It is essential to recognize that relapses are a normal part of the process and not a sign of failure.

Signs of a Digital Relapse

Increased Screen Time:

Noticing a significant increase in screen time, especially on non-essential activities, can indicate a relapse.

Neglecting Responsibilities:

When digital activities start to interfere with work, school, or personal responsibilities, it is a sign of problematic use.

Social Withdrawal:

Preferring online interactions over face-to-face communication can be a symptom of digital addiction resurfacing.

Emotional Triggers:

Feeling anxious, restless, or irritable when not using digital devices can signify dependency.

Addressing Setbacks

Acknowledge the Relapse:

The first step in addressing a relapse is to acknowledge it without self-judgment. Understanding that relapses are part of the journey helps in addressing them constructively (Marlatt & Donovan, 2005).

Identify Triggers:

Reflect on what triggered the relapse. Was it a specific event, emotion, or environment? Identifying triggers can help in developing strategies to avoid or manage them in the future (Sinha, 2001).

Revisit Goals:

Reevaluate your goals for digital wellness. Remind yourself why you started this journey and what you aim to achieve. This can provide motivation to get back on track.

Adjust Your Plan:

Based on your reflection, adjust your digital wellness plan. Implement new strategies or tools that can help prevent future relapses.

Seek Support:

Don't hesitate to seek support from friends, family, or professionals. Sharing your struggles and seeking advice can provide encouragement and new perspectives (Bandura, 1997).

Strategies for Long-Term Success

Maintaining digital wellness is a long-term commitment that requires consistent effort and adaptation. Here are strategies to support long-term success:

Consistent Self-Monitoring

Regularly monitor your digital habits to stay aware of your usage patterns. Use tools and apps that provide insights into screen time and app usage. Self-monitoring can help you catch potential relapses early and take corrective action (LaRose, Lin, & Eastin, 2003).

Setting Realistic Boundaries

Set and maintain realistic boundaries for digital use. This includes defining specific times for digital activities and ensuring you adhere to these limits.

Over time, these boundaries will become second nature and help prevent excessive use (Turkle, 2015).

Incorporating Mindfulness

Practice mindfulness to stay present and aware of your digital habits. Mindfulness can help you recognize when you are mindlessly engaging with technology and allow you to make more intentional choices. Techniques such as meditation and mindful breathing can be beneficial (Kabat-Zinn, 1990).

Diversifying Activities

Engage in a variety of offline activities to reduce reliance on digital devices. Pursue hobbies, spend time with loved ones, and participate in physical activities.

Diversifying your activities can help create a balanced lifestyle that does not revolve around technology (Csikszentmihalyi, 1996).

Regular Digital Detoxes

Schedule regular digital detoxes, where you disconnect from all digital devices for a set period. This can be a few hours each day, a full day each week, or even longer. Digital detoxes help reset your relationship with technology and remind you of the joys of offline life (Newport, 2019).

Building a Support System

Develop a support system of friends, family, or communities who share your goals for digital wellness. Having a support network can provide encouragement, accountability, and a sense of belonging. Participate in discussions, share experiences, and support each other's efforts (Bandura, 1997).

Continuing Education

Stay informed about the latest research and strategies for digital wellness. Read books, attend workshops, and follow experts in the field. Continuing education can provide new insights and keep you motivated on your journey (Turkle, 2015).

Creating a Positive Digital Environment

Curate a positive digital environment by following accounts and consuming content that inspires and uplifts you. Avoid content that triggers negative emotions or promotes unhealthy habits. A positive digital environment can enhance your overall well-being and support your goals (Rosen, 2012).

Kindly note here that the journey to digital wellness is ongoing. With persistence and adaptability, you can achieve a healthier relationship with technology. By recognizing and addressing setbacks and implementing strategies for long-term success, you can maintain a balanced digital routine.

Part V:

Special Consideration

Chapter 11

Digital Balance For Families

Maintaining digital balance within families is crucial for fostering healthy relationships and ensuring the well-being of all family members. This chapter provides guidance on helping children and teenagers develop healthy digital habits and offers strategies for setting family digital policies.

Guiding Children and Teenagers

Understanding the Impact of Technology on Youth

Children and teenagers are particularly susceptible to the effects of excessive screen time. Studies have shown that high levels of screen time can lead to various negative outcomes, including decreased physical activity, impaired social skills, and increased risk of mental health issues such as anxiety and depression (Twenge, 2017).

Therefore, guiding young people towards a balanced digital life is essential.

Strategies for Guiding Digital Use

Role Modelling:

Children often mimic the behaviours of their parents. By demonstrating healthy digital habits, parents can set a positive example. Limit your own screen time, engage in offline activities, and prioritize face-to-face interactions.

Open Communication:

Maintain open and honest communication about the benefits and risks of technology. Discuss the importance of balance and encourage children to share their experiences and feelings about their digital use.

Educational Content:

Encourage the use of educational apps and content that promote learning and creativity. Highlight the value of using technology for constructive purposes rather than passive consumption.

Screen Time Limits:

Set appropriate screen time limits based on the age and needs of the child. The American Academy of Pediatrics recommends no more than one hour of screen time per day for children aged 2 to 5, and consistent limits for older children and teenagers (AAP, 2016).

Promote Offline Activities:

Encourage participation in offline activities such as sports, reading, arts and crafts, and family outings. These activities help develop well-rounded individuals and reduce reliance on digital devices.

Teach Digital Citizenship:

Educate children about responsible and respectful online behaviour. Discuss topics such as cyber bullying, privacy, and the importance of critical thinking when consuming online content.

Parental Controls:

Utilize parental control tools to monitor and manage your children's digital activities. These tools can help enforce screen time limits, filter inappropriate content, and provide insights into usage patterns.

Setting Family Digital Policies

Creating a Family Agreement

Establishing a family digital policy can help create a unified approach to technology use. A family agreement sets clear expectations and guidelines for all members, promoting a healthy digital environment.

Components of a Family Digital Policy

Defined Screen Time:

Set clear limits on screen time for all family members. Specify the amount of time allowed for various activities, such as educational use, entertainment, and social media.

Screen-Free Zones and Times:

Designate specific areas of the home and times of day as screen-free. For example, make the dining room and bedrooms screen-free zones, and establish screen-free hours during meals and before bedtime.

Balanced Activities:

Ensure that the family engages in a variety of activities that do not involve screens. Plan regular family outings, game nights, and other offline activities that foster connection and fun.

Tech-Free Meals:

Prioritize family meals as opportunities for meaningful conversation and bonding. Make it a rule to keep all devices away from the dining table.

Bedtime Routines:

Create a calming bedtime routine that excludes screens. Encourage activities such as reading, journaling, or listening to calming music before bed to promote better sleep.

Shared Responsibilities:

Involve all family members in setting and maintaining the digital policy. Encourage children and teenagers to contribute their ideas and preferences, ensuring that the policy is fair and inclusive.

Regular Check-Ins:

Schedule regular family meetings to discuss how the digital policy is working. Use these check-ins to address any concerns, make adjustments, and celebrate successes.

Implementing and Enforcing the Policy

Consistency:

Consistently enforce the family digital policy to ensure that it becomes a natural part of daily life. Consistency helps establish clear expectations and reduces conflicts over screen time.

Positive Reinforcement:

Use positive reinforcement to encourage adherence to the policy. Praise and reward family members for following the guidelines and making healthy digital choices.

Lead by Example:

As parents, it is essential to adhere to the family digital policy. Demonstrating commitment to the guidelines reinforces their importance and encourages children to do the same.

Adaptability:

Be open to adjusting the policy as needed. Family dynamics and technology use may change over time, so it's important to remain flexible and make necessary updates to the guidelines.

Guiding children and teenagers towards healthy digital habits and establishing a comprehensive family digital policy, families can create a balanced and supportive environment for all members. These strategies help foster meaningful connections, promote well-being, and ensure that technology enhances rather than detracts from family life.

Chapter 12

Elderly and Digital Literacy

As technology becomes increasingly integral to daily life, fostering digital literacy among seniors is essential for promoting their well-being and ensuring they benefit from the digital age. This chapter focuses on encouraging healthy internet use among the elderly and addressing issues of isolation and digital addiction.

Encouraging Healthy Internet Use Among Seniors

Understanding the Digital Divide

Many elderly individuals face a digital divide, characterized by limited access to or proficiency with digital technologies. The digital divide can impact their ability to engage with online resources, access services, and stay connected with family and friends.

Bridging this divide requires targeted efforts to promote digital literacy and ensure that seniors can use technology effectively and safely.

Strategies for Encouraging Healthy Internet Use

Provide Basic Training:

Offer workshops or one-on-one training sessions that cover basic digital skills. Topics might include using a computer or smart phone, navigating the internet, and understanding online safety.

Community centers, libraries, and senior organizations can be valuable resources for such training (Hargittai & Dobransky, 2017).

Promote Online Safety:

Educate seniors about online safety and security. This includes recognizing phishing scams, creating strong passwords, and understanding privacy settings.

Providing clear, easy-to-follow guidelines can help seniors navigate the digital world more confidently.

Encourage Social Connections:

Use technology to foster social connections and combat loneliness. Encourage seniors to use video calls, social media, and messaging apps to stay in touch with family and friends. Platforms like Zoom, Facebook, and WhatsApp can help maintain social ties and provide opportunities for virtual interaction (Cotten, 2013).

Introduce Useful Apps:

Introduce seniors to apps and online services that can enhance their daily lives. This might include health management apps, online shopping, and entertainment options. Demonstrating practical applications of technology can make digital tools more relevant and appealing.

Offer Ongoing Support:

Provide continuous support and assistance as seniors become more comfortable with technology. Create support groups or helplines where they can ask questions and receive help with digital issues.

Simplify Technology:

Opt for devices and software designed with seniors in mind. Many technology companies offer simplified versions of devices and applications that cater to older adults, with larger fonts, easy navigation, and user-friendly interfaces.

Addressing Isolation and Digital Addiction

Understanding the Risks

While technology can help alleviate isolation, it can also lead to digital addiction, particularly if not used mindfully.

Seniors may become overly reliant on digital devices for social interaction, potentially leading to further isolation from in-person relationships and activities.

Strategies to Address Isolation and Digital Addiction

Promote Balanced Use:

Encourage a balanced approach to technology use. While it's beneficial for seniors to use technology to connect with others, it's equally important to engage in offline activities and face-to-face interactions. Create a schedule that includes both digital and non-digital activities.

Encourage Participation in Community Activities: Facilitate participation in local community events and activities. This helps seniors engage with their physical community and build relationships beyond the digital realm. Community centers, clubs, and local organizations can offer opportunities for social engagement.

Monitor and Limit Screen Time:

Help seniors set reasonable limits on screen time to prevent digital addiction. Establish specific times for using technology and encourage breaks to engage in other activities. Monitoring screen time can help maintain a healthy balance.

Facilitate Family Involvement:

Involve family members in the process of digital integration. Family members can provide support, encourage healthy habits, and participate in activities that combine digital and in-person interactions.

Offer Educational Programs:

Provide educational programs that focus on digital wellness and the impacts of excessive screen time. Workshops or seminars can help seniors understand the importance of balancing digital use with other aspects of life.

Create Opportunities for Offline Activities:

Offer or recommend activities that do not involve technology, such as art classes, gardening, or physical exercise. Engaging in offline activities can provide a well-rounded lifestyle and help mitigate the risks of digital addiction.

Encourage Mindfulness:

Teach mindfulness practices to help seniors become more aware of their digital habits and the impact of technology on their well-being. Mindfulness techniques can promote a more intentional and balanced approach to digital use (Creswell, 2017).

Fostering digital literacy among seniors and addressing issues of isolation and digital addiction require a multifaceted approach.

Providing basic training, promoting online safety, and encouraging balanced use of technology, can help the elderly navigate the digital world effectively.

Additionally, addressing isolation and preventing digital addiction involve creating opportunities for meaningful offline interactions and supporting a balanced lifestyle.

Appendices

These resources and tools are designed to support readers in their journey towards digital balance and well-being.

Appendix A: Resources for Further Reading

Books

"Digital Minimalism: Choosing a Focused Life in a Noisy World" by Cal Newport (2019)

This book explores the benefits of simplifying digital use and offers practical strategies for living a more focused life.

"Reclaiming Conversation: The Power of Talk in a Digital Age" by Sherry Turkle (2015)

Turkle examines how digital communication impacts our relationships and provides insights into fostering meaningful conversations.

"The Shallows: What the Internet Is Doing to Our Brains" by Nicholas Carr (2010)

Carr discusses how constant internet use affects cognitive function and the implications for mental health and productivity.

"Digital Detox: The Ultimate Guide to Beating Technology Addiction" by Simon & Schuster (2021)

Articles and Research Papers

This guide offers strategies and tips for managing technology use and reducing dependency on digital devices.

"The Impact of Internet Addiction on Sleep Quality: A Review" by Lu, H., & Lee, S. (2019) in Sleep Medicine Reviews, 43, 64-73.

A review of how excessive internet use affects sleep quality and overall health.

"Digital Detox and Well-being: A Review of the Literature" by M. Griffiths (2020) in Journal of Behavioral Addictions, 9(1), 12-21.

Websites and Online Resources

This paper reviews the literature on digital detox practices and their effects on mental well-being.

Center for Humane Technology: https://www.humanetech.com

Provides resources and information on technology's impact on society and ways to promote a healthier digital environment.

Digital Detox: https://www.digitaldetox.org

Offers information on digital detox strategies, workshops, and tools for managing technology use.

Appendix B: Support and Counseling Services

National Helplines and Support Services

National Suicide Prevention Lifeline: 1-800-273-TALK (8255)

Provides free and confidential support 24/7 for those in distress or crisis.

Crisis Text Line: Text "HELLO" to 741741

Offers free, confidential support via text for individuals in crisis.

Counselling and Therapy Services

Psychology Today Therapy Directory: https://www.psychologytoday.com/us/therapists

A directory to find licensed therapists and counselors specializing in digital addiction and mental health issues.

BetterHelp: https://www.betterhelp.com

An online platform offering access to licensed therapists for virtual counseling sessions.

Local and Community Support Groups

Local Senior Centers and Community Organizations: Contact local senior centers or community organizations for support groups and workshops on digital literacy and well-being.

Digital Wellness Network: https://www.digitalwellness.org

Offers information on digital wellness, including local support groups and educational resources.

Appendix C: Self-Help Tools and Worksheets

Digital Usage Tracker

Description: A tool to monitor and record daily digital usage. Helps identify patterns and areas where adjustments are needed.

Sample Tracker: Include columns for date, device used, time spent, and activity description.

Digital Detox Plan Worksheet

Description: A worksheet to create a personalized digital detox plan, including goals, strategies, and action steps.

Sections:

Goals: Define specific objectives for reducing screen time and improving digital habits.

Strategies: Outline methods and techniques to achieve the goals.

Action Steps: Create a detailed plan with timelines and checkpoints.

Mindfulness and Reflection Journal

Description: A journal to practice mindfulness and reflect on digital habits and their impact on well-being.

Sections:

Daily Reflections: Space to write about daily experiences, feelings, and observations related to digital use.

Mindfulness Exercises: Include prompts for mindfulness practices, such as deep breathing or meditation.

Screen Time Management Plan

Description: A plan to manage and balance screen time, including setting limits and scheduling offline activities.

Daily Schedule: Create a daily schedule that includes time for work, leisure, and offline activities.

Screen Time Limits: Set specific limits for different types of digital activities (e.g., social media, work).

Family Digital Policy Template

Description: A template to develop a family digital policy, including guidelines and rules for technology use.

Sections:

Screen Time Limits: Define limits for each family member.

Screen-Free Zones: Designate areas and times where digital devices are not allowed.

Family Activities: List offline activities that the family can engage in together.

References

Cited Works

Journal of Behavioral Addictions. "Global Prevalence of Internet Addiction: A Meta-Analysis." [Link to study]

Cheng, C., & Li, A. Y. (2014). Internet addiction prevalence and quality of (real) life: A meta-analysis of 31 nations across seven world regions. Cyberpsychology, Behavior, and Social Networking, 17(12), 755-760.

Griffiths, M. (1998). Internet addiction: Does it really exist? In J. Gackenbach (Ed.), Psychology and the Internet: Intrapersonal, Interpersonal, and Transpersonal Implications (pp. 61-75). Academic Press.

Hershner, S., & Chervin, R. (2014). Causes and consequences of sleepiness among college students. Nature and Science of Sleep, 6, 73-84.

Kuss, D. J., Griffiths, M. D., & Binder, J. F. (2014). Internet addiction in students: Prevalence and risk factors. Computers in Human Behaviour, 29(3), 959-966.

Kraut, R., Patterson, M., Lundmark, V., Kiesler, S., Mukopadhyay, T., & Scherlis, W. (1998). Internet paradox: A social technology that reduces social involvement and psychological well-being? American Psychologist, 53(9), 1017-1031.

Lin, M. P., Wu, J. Y. W., You, J., Hu, W. H., & Yen, C. F. (2016). Prevalence of internet addiction and its risk and protective factors in a representative sample of senior high school students in Taiwan. Journal of Adolescence, 43, 50-58.

Shariat, A., Cleland, J. A., Danaee, M., Kargarfard, M., Sangelaji, B., & Tamrin, S. B. M. (2018).

Effects of stretching exercise training and ergonomic modifications on musculoskeletal discomforts of office workers: A randomized controlled trial. Brazilian Journal of Physical Therapy, 22, 144-153.

Sheppard, A. L., & Wolffsohn, J. S. (2018). Digital eye strain: prevalence, measurement and amelioration. BMJ Open Ophthalmology, 3(1), e000146.

Swing, E. L., Gentile, D. A., Anderson, C. A., & Walsh, D. A. (2010). Television and video game exposure and the development of attention problems. Pediatrics, 126(2), 214-221.

Young, K. S. (1998). Caught in the Net: How to Recognize the Signs of Internet Addiction--and a Winning Strategy for Recovery. John Wiley & Sons.

Young, K. S. (2004). Internet addiction: A new clinical phenomenon and its consequences American Behavioral Scientist, 48(4), 402-415.

Hofmann, W., Vohs, K. D., & Baumeister, R. F. (2012). What people desire, feel conflicted about, and try to resist in everyday life. Psychological Science, 23(6), 582-588.

Meerkerk, G. J., Van Den Eijnden, R. J., Vermulst, A. A., & Garretsen, H. F. (2009). The Compulsive Internet Use Scale (CIUS): Some psychometric properties. CyberPsychology & Behavior, 12(1), 1-6.

Young, K. S. (1998). Caught in the Net: How to Recognize the Signs of Internet Addiction--and a Winning Strategy for Recovery. John Wiley & Sons.

Andreassen, C. S., Pallesen, S., & Griffiths, M. D. (2017).

The relationship between addictive use of social media, narcissism, and self-esteem: Findings from a large national survey. Addictive Behaviours, 64, 287-293.

Billieux, J., Maurage, P., Lopez-Fernandez, O., Kuss, D. J., & Griffiths, M. D. (2015). Can disordered mobile phone use be considered a behavioural addiction? An update on current evidence and a comprehensive model for future research. Current Addiction Reports, 2(2), 156-162.

Caplan, S. E. (2007). Relations among loneliness, social anxiety, and problematic internet use. CyberPsychology & Behavior, 10(2), 234-242.

Carr, N. (2010). The Shallows: What the Internet Is Doing to Our Brains. W. W. Norton & Company.

Kraut, R., Patterson, M., Lundmark, V., Kiesler, S., Mukopadhyay, T., & Scherlis, W. (1998). Internet paradox:

A social technology that reduces social involvement and psychological well-being? American Psychologist, 53(9), 1017-1031.

Lam, L. T., & Peng, Z. W. (2010). Effect of pathological use of the internet on adolescent mental health: A prospective study. Archives of Pediatrics & Adolescent Medicine, 164(10), 901-906.

Lin, M. P., Wu, J. Y. W., You, J., Hu, W. H., & Yen, C. F. (2016). Prevalence of internet addiction and its risk and protective factors in a representative sample of senior high school students in Taiwan. Journal of Adolescence, 43, 50-58.

Montag, C., Lachmann, B., Herrlich, M., & Zweig, K. (2019). Addictive features of social media/messenger platforms and freemium games against the background of psychological and economic theories. International Journal of Environmental Research and Public Health, 16(14), 2612.

Przybylski, A. K., Murayama, K., DeHaan, C. R., & Gladwell, V. (2013). Motivational, emotional, and behavioral correlates of fear of missing out. Computers in Human Behavior, 29(4), 1841-1848.

Wilson, E. O. (2014). The Meaning of Human Existence. Liveright Publishing.

American Academy of Pediatrics (AAP). (2016). Media and Young Minds. Pediatrics, 138(5), e20162591.

Cash, H., Rae, C. D., Steel, A. H., & Winkler, A. (2012). Internet Addiction: A Brief Summary of Research and Practice. Current Psychiatry Reviews, 8(4), 292-298.

Mark, G., Gudith, D., & Klocke, U. (2008). The Cost of Interrupted Work: More Speed and Stress. Proceedings of the SIGCHI Conference on Human Factors in Computing Systems, 107-110.

National Sleep Foundation (NSF). (2011). Technology Use and Sleep. Sleep in America Poll.

Wilmer, H. H., Sherman, L. E., & Chein, J. M. (2017). Smartphones and Cognition: A Review of Research Exploring the Links between Mobile Technology Habits and Cognitive Functioning. Frontiers in Psychology, 8, 605.

Chun, M. M., Golomb, J. D., & Turk-Browne, N. B. (2011). A taxonomy of external and internal attention. Annual Review of Psychology, 62, 73-101.

Davis, D. M., & Hayes, J. A. (2011). What are the benefits of mindfulness? A practice review of psychotherapy-related research. Psychotherapy, 48(2), 198-208.

Newport, C. (2019). Digital Minimalism: Choosing a Focused Life in a Noisy World. Portfolio.

Ophir, E., Nass, C., & Wagner, A. D. (2009). Cognitive control in media multitaskers. Proceedings of the National Academy of Sciences, 106(37), 15583-15587.

Rosenfield, M. (2011). Computer vision syndrome: a review of ocular causes and potential treatments. Ophthalmic and Physiological Optics, 31(5), 502-515.

Vogel, E. A., Rose, J. P., Roberts, L. R., & Eckles, K. (2014). Social comparison, social media, and self-esteem. Psychology of Popular Media Culture, 3(4), 206-222.

Brownell, J. (2012). Listening: Attitudes, Principles, and Skills (5th ed.). Pearson.

Csikszentmihalyi, M. (1996). Creativity: Flow and the Psychology of Discovery and Invention. HarperCollins.

Dunbar, R. I. M. (2010). The social role of touch in humans and primates: Behavioural function and neurobiological mechanisms. Neuroscience & Biobehavioral Reviews, 34(2), 260-268.

Gottman, J., & Silver, N. (1999). The Seven Principles for Making Marriage Work. Three Rivers Press.

Holt-Lunstad, J., Smith, T. B., & Layton, J. B. (2010). Social relationships and mortality risk: A meta-analytic review. PLOS Medicine, 7(7), e1000316.

Newport, C. (2019). Digital Minimalism: Choosing a Focused Life in a Noisy World. Portfolio.

Pressman, S. D., Matthews, K. A., Cohen, S., Martire, L. M., Scheier, M., Baum, A., & Schulz, R. (2009). Association of enjoyable leisure activities with psychological and physical well-being. Psychosomatic Medicine, 71(7), 725-732.

Turkle, S. (2015). Reclaiming Conversation: The Power of Talk in a Digital Age. Penguin Press.

Warburton, D. E., Nicol, C. W., & Bredin, S. S. (2006). Health benefits of physical activity: The evidence. Canadian Medical Association Journal, 174(6), 801-809.

Newport, C. (2019). Digital Minimalism: Choosing a Focused Life in a Noisy World. Portfolio.

Puddicombe, A. (2016). The Headspace Guide to Meditation and Mindfulness. St. Martin's Griffin.

Rosen, L. D. (2012). iDisorder: Understanding Our Obsession with Technology and Overcoming Its Hold on Us. Palgrave Macmillan.

Tsekleves, E., & Cooper, R. (2017). Technology and Wellbeing. In Design for Health (pp. 111-129). Routledge.

Books written by the Author

- *Body, Mind, and Fuel: The Triad of Total Fitness*

- *The Soccer Oracle:*

  Mastering Predictions and Betting Strategies

- *Decoding Blockchain: Mastering the Crypto Revolution*

- *Mindful Living: Unleash Your Power Within*

- *Positive Psychology and Happiness*

- *Mental Health and Well-being: A Path to Balance*

- *The Path to a Perfect Marriage: A Guide*

- *Africa, Be Wise*

- *Journey to Inner Peace: Healing the Human Soul*

All these can be seen @ https://franknwaorie.com/books